Sitting Bull

History Maker Bios

Susan Bivin Aller

LERNER PUBLICATIONS COMPANY • MINNEAPOLIS

The publisher would like to thank Holly A. Annis for her assistance with this book.

Illustrations by Tim Parlin

The details of Sitting Bull's life vary across sources. the primary source used for this book was Robert M. Utley's *The Lance and the Sheild: The Life and Times of Sitting Bull*. Sitting Bull's speeches quoted in this book are translations.

Lerner Publications Company
A division of Lerner Publishing Group
241 First Avenue North
Minneapolis, MN 55401 U.S.A.

Website address: www.lernerbooks.com

Library of Congress Cataloging-in-Publication Data

Aller, Susan Bivin.
    Sitting Bull / by Susan Bivin Aller.
      p.   cm. — (History maker bios)
    Summary: Introduces the life of Lakota Sioux warrior and holy man Sitting Bull, who led his people to victory at Little Bighorn and brought them to safety in Canada before surrendering so that they would not starve.
    Includes bibliographical references and index.
    ISBN-13: 978–0–8225–0700–0 (lib. bdg. : alk. paper)
    ISBN-10: 0–8225–0700–5 (lib. bdg. : alk. paper)
    1. Sitting Bull, 1834?–1890—Juvenile literature. 2. Dakota Indians—Kings and rulers—Biography—Juvenile literature. 3. Hunkpapa Indians—Kings and rulers—Biography—Juvenile literature. 4. Little Bighorn, Battle of the, Mont., 1876—Juvenile literature. [1. Sitting Bull, 1834?–1890. 2. Dakota Indians— Biography. 3. Hunkpapa Indians—Biography. 4. Indians of North America— Great Plains—Biography. 5. Kings, queens, rulers, etc. 6. Little Bighorn, Battle of the, Mont., 1876.] I. Title. II. Series.
E99.D1S463 2004
978.004'975244'0092—dc22   2003012168

Manufactured in the United States of America
2 3 4 5 6 7 – JR – 11 10 09 08 07 06

TABLE OF CONTENTS

INTRODUCTION 5

1. A BOY CALLED SLOW 6

2. A CHANGING WORLD 14

3. FIGHTING FOR FREEDOM 20

4. SITTING BULL'S VISION 29

5. LIVING FOR HIS PEOPLE 36

TIMELINE 44

SHOWMAN 45

FURTHER READING 46

WEBSITES 46

SELECT BIBLIOGRAPHY 47

INDEX 48

INTRODUCTION

Sitting Bull was one of the greatest spiritual leaders and warriors of the Lakota people. He lived with his people on the Great Plains of the Dakota Territory from about 1831 to 1890.

Sitting Bull believed the Great Spirit chose him to lead and protect his people. He was brave, generous, and wise. To the end of his life, Sitting Bull defended the Lakota's right to live freely and peacefully on their homelands.

This is his story.

1 A BOY CALLED SLOW

A young Hunkpapa boy raced his friends across the grassy plain. His nickname was Hunkesni, which meant "Slow." But he almost always won a race. Everyone called him Slow because he took his time deciding to do something. He thought before he spoke. Slow was also stubborn. He never let go of what he held.

One day, when Slow was ten years old, he and his friends went buffalo hunting. Slow dug his feet into the sides of his pony and galloped toward a buffalo herd. His friends tried to catch up with him, but their ponies weren't fast enough. Slow rode swiftly toward a buffalo calf and its mother. He shot an arrow at the calf and brought it down. Slow had made his first buffalo kill.

Slow brought the calf home. But his father told him to give it to a family who needed food. He wanted his son to be generous and to share with other people. Generosity was one of the most important lessons Slow could learn. He never forgot it.

Millions of buffalo, or bison, grazed on the plains when Slow was young.

The Hunkpapa Lakota lived in tipis covered with buffalo skin. Slow was probably born in one like this about 1831.

Slow grew up on the Grand River in north-central South Dakota. His family belonged to the Hunkpapa people. The Hunkpapas were one of the seven bands of Lakota people. The Lakota were sometimes called the Teton Sioux. Their homelands were the Great Plains of North Dakota, South Dakota, Nebraska, Wyoming, and Montana.

When Slow was young, there were no towns or roads on the Great Plains. Few white people lived there, either—except for fur traders. But millions of buffalo and many other animals, such as deer and bear, roamed the plains. Slow learned to hunt these animals with his bow and arrow. He also caught fish in the streams and learned how to collect the best fruits and berries.

THE LAKOTA AND THE BUFFALO

The Lakota depended on the buffalo. Buffalo meat was their main food. They made tipis, clothing, and tools from the skin and bones of buffalo. And dried buffalo manure was used to build fires. Every spring and fall, millions of buffalo migrated, or moved, from one part of the plains to another. They were trying to find fresh grass to eat. When the buffalo migrated, the Lakota people took down their tipis and packed their belongings. They followed the buffalo to new hunting grounds.

Slow learned to copy the calls of birds, like the sound of the hawk.

Like other Hunkpapa children, Slow grew up with a large and loving group of grown-ups to teach and guide him. He was taught to be kind to others and to respect the earth. He learned that everything—the buffalo, the eagle, the sun, the sky, the earth, and the wind—had a spirit and was connected to Wakan Tanka, or the Great Spirit. Wakan Tanka had created and was a part of everything sacred. Slow learned to honor these spirits. He seemed especially close to them. He said he could understand the language of birds and other animals.

Slow also learned how to fight. He wanted to become a warrior like his father. Hunkpapa men were proud and honorable warriors. When the Hunkpapas won a battle, they captured their enemies' horses. The number of horses a man had showed how good a warrior he was. A Hunkpapa also earned honors by being the first person to touch an enemy. This was called counting coup. Coup (KOO) is the French word for a strike or blow.

One day, Slow's father and some other men went to defend the village against an enemy band of Crow warriors. Slow was only fourteen years old, but he joined the war party.

Lakota warriors earned honors in battle by touching their enemies with a coup stick.

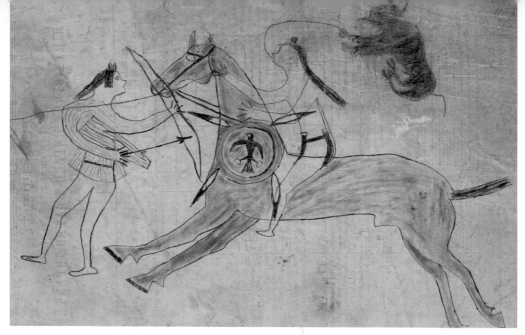

Sitting Bull drew a pictograph like this of himself counting his first coup against a Crow warrior.

The Hunkpapas hid behind a ridge until they saw some Crow warriors coming. Then they began to charge toward the Crows. Slow did not wait for the other men. He went ahead. The older men followed him, yelling and waving their weapons. The Crow warriors tried to get away, but Slow caught up with one of them and knocked him off his horse. He was the first to hit the enemy. He had counted coup. Slow had proved that he was brave. He wasn't afraid to get close to an enemy.

That night, the Hunkpapas celebrated the victory with a feast for the whole camp. Slow was the hero. Slow's father put a white eagle feather in his son's hair and gave him a horse.

Then Slow's father presented his young warrior son with a shield of buffalo hide. He also gave Slow a long wooden lance, or spear, with an iron blade. Slow treasured these special gifts.

Finally, Slow's father gave him a new name. It was Tatanka Iyotake, or "Sitting Bull." The name meant someone powerful and stubborn—like a huge seated buffalo bull that couldn't be moved.

2 A CHANGING WORLD

S itting Bull grew into a strong young man. He was nearly six feet tall with powerful arms. He could shoot his arrows and throw his lance with great force.

Sitting Bull earned many honors for his courage in battle. When he was twenty-five, he was shot through the foot by a Crow warrior. The wound made him limp when he walked. But Sitting Bull was fast and graceful on his horse.

The Hunkpapas admired Sitting Bull because he was wise and kind. They looked up to him as an important spiritual leader. He had a special gift. He could understand the meaning of dreams. Sometimes he received visions from the spirit world. Sitting Bull felt that Wakan Tanka chose him to use his gifts to help his people.

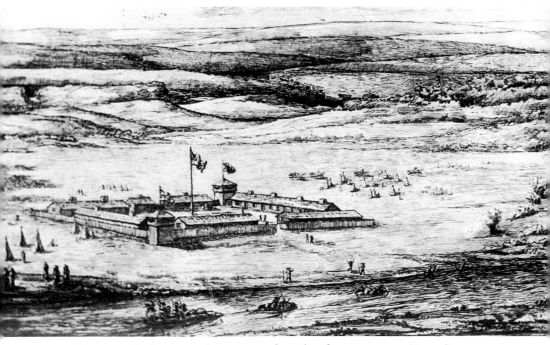

Sitting Bull saw white men for the first time at Fort Pierre, South Dakota. Every year, the Hunkpapas went there to trade buffalo hides for white people's goods.

When Sitting Bull was a young man, white settlers from the East began moving to the Great Plains. The Hunkpapas didn't know anything about the settlers. Sitting Bull watched with curiosity as covered wagons rolled over the grassy plains. The wagons brought the white settlers. Over the years, more and more white people came. Sitting Bull began to worry about the safety of his people.

Thousands of wagons carrying white settlers carved trails through Lakota lands.

White settlers cut down trees to build houses and fences. They plowed up the land to plant crops. Their cattle and other livestock ate the prairie grasses that the buffalo needed for grazing. When the buffalo left to find more grass, the Hunkpapas had to follow them.

Giving Away Native American Lands

In 1862, President Abraham Lincoln signed two acts into law. The Pacific Railroad Act gave millions of acres of land to railway companies. These companies built a railroad and a telegraph line from the Missouri River to the Pacific Ocean. The Homestead Act gave away pieces of valuable land called homesteads. After five years of living and farming on a piece of land, the homesteader owned the land. The United States called the land it gave away "public land." But the land was already home to Native Americans.

Sitting Bull and his people were defeated by U.S. soldiers at the Battle of Killdeer Mountain in 1864.

The Hunkpapas saw these white settlers as invaders of their land. The settlers used the best parts of the land. They left the Hunkpapas with few places to live and hunt.

The Hunkpapas decided to fight back. Sitting Bull and his Hunkpapa warriors attacked wagon trains, forts, and settlements. Other Plains Indians joined the attacks. They tried to make the white people leave.

The white people were frightened. Some left or were killed, but more settlers kept coming. Many fought back. They said the government had given them the land. But Sitting Bull and his people wondered how anyone could own what Wakan Tanka had given to all people.

The United States tried to make the settlements safe. The government sent soldiers to protect the settlers. But the fighting continued.

3 FIGHTING FOR FREEDOM

I n 1868, the U.S. government had a plan to stop all the fighting on the Great Plains. Sitting Bull and other Plains Indian leaders had their own demands for peace. They wanted the government to close its roads and railways, to burn its forts, and to stop steamboat traffic on the rivers. They wanted all white people, except traders, to move off of the land.

The U.S. government said Sitting Bull's demands were impossible. Settlers needed even more land. The government offered to buy land from the Hunkpapas and other Plains Indians. The government presented a treaty, or agreement, for them to sign. Some leaders signed, but Sitting Bull refused.

Government agents and leaders of the Plains Indians sign the Fort Laramie Treaty of 1868. Sitting Bull would not sign it.

Government agents (CENTER) were in charge of handing out food and clothing on reservations.

The treaty set aside a large piece of protected land that already belonged to the Plains Indians. It was to be called the Great Sioux Reservation. No white settlers would be allowed to live there. Leaders who signed the treaty agreed to move their people on to the reservation. They would stop traveling over the plains to hunt and fight. In return, the government would give them money, food, and clothing every year.

Sitting Bull thought the reservation sounded like a prison. He wanted to be free to move about on his lands without worrying about white people. So he led the Hunkpapas and other Lakota bands farther west into Montana. The government didn't like that. It called Sitting Bull's people "hostile," or unfriendly. Most people called them the hunting bands because they continued to hunt buffalo to live.

RESERVATIONS

On the reservation, the Lakota were forced to live like white people. But they didn't have the same rights as whites. They couldn't hunt. Instead, they raised cattle and planted crops. They wore clothes that white people wore. Children were often taken away from their families and sent to boarding school. At school, they were not allowed to speak Lakota. They learned to read and write only English.

Sitting Bull speaks to his followers.

As Sitting Bull became more famous, the Hunkpapas and other hunting bands elected him leader of the Lakota nation. He was about thirty-eight years old. The U.S. government also recognized Sitting Bull as a powerful man. He could speak for all the Lakota in times of war and peace.

Even in Montana, Sitting Bull couldn't get away from white people. Surveyors were mapping the route for a new railroad. A few years later, in 1872, the surveyors went into the valley of the Yellowstone River—not far from where Sitting Bull lived. Several hundred soldiers went with the surveyors to protect them.

Sitting Bull didn't want to fight, but some of his younger warriors did. They formed a war party and rode out to do battle with the soldiers. Just as the shooting began, Sitting Bull walked into the line of fire between the soldiers and the Lakota warriors. He sat down on the ground, took out his pipe, and began to smoke it. The soldiers and the warriors were amazed at Sitting Bull's courage.

Sitting Bull called out for others to come and smoke with him. Four men joined him, but they were very nervous. Bullets flew around them. When the five men had smoked the pipe, Sitting Bull calmly got up and walked back to his warriors. Then he shouted out to them that there had been enough fighting. He ordered them to quit and go home. So they did. The soldiers also quit fighting. And the surveyors left the Yellowstone River valley.

Sitting Bull's council pipe

The army realized it would have trouble getting the railroad through Sitting Bull's lands. In 1873, it sent in more troops. One of the first units to arrive was the Seventh U.S. Cavalry. Its commander was a young lieutenant colonel named George Armstrong Custer. The Plains Indians called him "Long Hair" because his red-gold hair hung down to his shoulders.

George Armstrong Custer (SEATED) with his Native American scouts. Custer led his cavalry into Lakota lands.

The Black Hills are holy mountains to the Lakota.

The government had a secret mission for Custer. They wanted him to take some miners into Paha Sapa, or the Black Hills, and look for gold. The Black Hills were part of the Great Sioux Reservation. They were holy mountains to Sitting Bull's people. The Lakota believed their nation had been created in the Black Hills. They believed that the sacred spirits of their people still lived there. The hills were also a good hunting place.

Custer's miners found gold there and started a gold rush. Thousands of gold seekers raced to the Black Hills, hoping to get rich. The Lakota were furious. White people had broken their promise to stay out of the Great Sioux Reservation. They had ignored the agreements of the treaty. And they had begun to dig in the sacred heart of the Black Hills.

The government tried to buy the Black Hills, but the Lakota said no. Sitting Bull told the Lakota to rise up and defend their land.

Custer's cavalry crosses the Great Plains of the Dakota Territory in 1874.

4 SITTING BULL'S VISION

In 1876, Sitting Bull called a war council. The United States had ordered all the hunting bands to turn themselves in to the reservation. The bands had refused. Because they said no, three armies were coming to take them in.

Lakota men sit for a council
meeting in 1891. Sitting Bull's
council may have looked
like this.

By spring,
thousands of Lakota,
Cheyenne, and Arapaho
people gathered near Sitting Bull's village
on Rosebud Creek. It was the largest camp
ever seen on the Great Plains. Around three
thousand people came. They also came to
take part in the Sun Dance—the most
important ceremony of the year.

Excitement ran high in the camp. Sitting
Bull's people looked to him for guidance.
He asked the spirits for help and prepared
to dance the Sun Dance. He had to give
some part of himself to the spirits. Then the
spirits would answer his prayers and help
to protect his people.

To prepare himself, Sitting Bull had his brother cut a hundred small pieces of flesh from his arms. Then, with blood flowing from his cuts, Sitting Bull began a slow, rhythmic dance. All the while, he stared directly at the blazing June sun. Sitting Bull had no food or water and was in great pain, but he kept on dancing. He danced for hours. Finally, he stopped and stood as if he were in a dream. Friends lowered him to the ground and sprinkled him with water. When he woke from his trance, he told his followers that Wakan Tanka had sent him the vision he prayed for.

This pictograph of the Sun Dance was drawn by Short Bull, a Lakota.

Gall (LEFT) and Crazy Horse joined Sitting Bull and led their people to the Little Bighorn River.

In his vision, Sitting Bull saw soldiers and horses—as numerous as grasshoppers—falling from the sky. The soldiers and horses were upside down. That meant they were dead. Sitting Bull said there was going to be a great battle. The hunting bands would win, and the white soldiers would be killed.

Thousands of people joined Sitting Bull's camp. There were about 7,000 people, including about 1,800 warriors. The camp moved every few days. They needed to find huge quantities of food and firewood for the people and fresh pastures for their horses. Their search for food led the camp to the Little Bighorn River.

On the night of June 24, Sitting Bull climbed to a ridge overlooking the river and the camp of a thousand tipis. He offered Wakan Tanka a buffalo robe, a sacred pipe, and bundles of tobacco. Then he prayed to Wakan Tanka to be with him and his people and to let them live.

THE END OF THE BUFFALO

For centuries, millions of buffalo lived on the Great Plains. They covered the plains as far as the eye could see. To force the Plains Indians onto reservations, the government decided to get rid of the buffalo. It hired sharpshooters, people who were skilled at shooting targets, to kill the buffalo. Between 1872 and 1874, these sharpshooters killed more than four million of the animals. By 1895, fewer than one thousand buffalo were left. Since then, people have tried hard to save the buffalo.

The next day, the Seventh U.S. Cavalry, led by "Long Hair" Custer, made a surprise attack on Sitting Bull's camp. Custer had only about 210 men with him. He didn't know that thousands of warriors had gathered at Sitting Bull's camp. Custer's soldiers charged the village. The warriors immediately surrounded them.

In a little over one hour, Custer and every one of his men were killed. The Battle of the Little Bighorn was over. Sitting Bull's vision had come true.

A Lakota drew this pictograph of the Battle of the Little Bighorn. Sitting Bull is the man standing on the far left of the four men in the center.

Americans were very angry that so many soldiers had been killed. They sent more cavalry units to kill the hunting bands or to force them onto reservations. Sitting Bull managed to avoid the soldiers for the rest of the year. But the Hunkpapas were hungry and had lost hope. Sitting Bull wanted to help his people. So he led them across the border and into Canada in May of 1877. In Canada, the United States Army could not arrest him.

5 LIVING FOR HIS PEOPLE

S itting Bull stayed in Canada for about four years. His people still hunted buffalo. But many of the herds had been killed off. It was hard to find enough to eat. In 1881, the Hunkpapas were starving. So Sitting Bull led his people back across the border. He was ready to turn himself in to the U.S. Army.

Crow Foot was Sitting Bull's favorite of his many children.

Sitting Bull handed his rifle to his favorite son, Crow Foot. The boy was five years old. Sitting Bull told his son to give it to the officer in charge. Then Sitting Bull spoke to the officer about the future. Sitting Bull did not trust white people, but he said that he wanted his children to learn from them. He also hoped his people could live freely on the Great Plains.

"I wish it to be remembered that I was the last man of my tribe to surrender my rifle," Sitting Bull said.

Sitting Bull and his followers were held prisoners at Fort Randall, South Dakota, for nearly two years. Then they were sent to the Standing Rock Agency. It was near Sitting Bull's birthplace on the Grand River. Sitting Bull was forced to become a farmer. He grew grains and vegetables and took care of cattle. He lived in a log house.

Sitting Bull sits with his wife Seen-by-the-Nation in 1882. They were prisoners at Fort Randall.

Sitting Bull (FAR LEFT) poses with other Native American leaders on a visit to Washington, D.C.

A government agent was hired to control the Hunkpapas. He watched Sitting Bull all the time. Sitting Bull was still a leader. And the U.S. government didn't want him to cause any more trouble.

Sitting Bull had become famous as the man who killed Custer at the Battle of the Little Bighorn. But Sitting Bull hadn't killed Custer. Sitting Bull was at the battle, but he didn't fight. The story made him a famous person anyway. Many people wanted to see him. Reporters interviewed him for their newspapers.

William F. Cody as *"Buffalo Bill"* in his Wild West Show

In 1885, the showman Buffalo Bill Cody wanted Sitting Bull to perform in his traveling Wild West Show. Buffalo Bill had to ask the agent if it was OK. The agent said yes. Sitting Bull spent only a few months with the show. But in that short time, he learned many things—both good and bad—about the white people's world. He did not want to live like white people.

Sitting Bull and his people felt that they had lost everything important to them except their lives. Their lands had been taken from them. They were forced to live like whites. Never again would the Hunkpapas roam freely to hunt the buffalo. Even the buffalo were gone.

Suddenly, a new religion spread through the Native American nations. It was called the Ghost Dance. In the Ghost Dance, people danced and prayed to Wakan Tanka. The dancers believed they were helping to bring about the end of the old world and the beginning of a new one. In the new world, there would be no white people. The buffalo would return, and Native Americans would live in peace on their lands forever.

Ghost Dancers hoped to bring peace and freedom to Native Americans.

In a short time, the Ghost Dance appeared at the Standing Rock Agency. The agent was afraid that Sitting Bull might cause trouble by encouraging the new religion. Sitting Bull did not dance, but he didn't tell his followers to stop. The agent told policemen to take Sitting Bull to a military jail until the Ghost Dance movement died down.

On December 15, 1890, forty-three Lakota policemen surrounded Sitting Bull's cabin. When he came out, they arrested him. A large group of his followers had come to see what was happening.

Two of Sitting Bull's wives, his two daughters, and a son stand in front of his tipi.

A shot was fired. It hit a policeman. More shots rang out, and in another minute, Sitting Bull lay dead. Several of his followers, including his young son Crow Foot, were also killed.

Sitting Bull lived his entire life for his people. He tried to keep the old way of life for his people even when it seemed impossible. He was brave, generous, and wise. He was also strong and stubborn. Sitting Bull had always lived up to his name.

THE LIVING LAKOTA

About 25,000 Lakota live on reservations in South Dakota. Many others live in towns and cities in North Dakota, South Dakota, Nebraska, and other states. All Lakota children on the reservation are taught the Lakota language, history, and culture. Sun Dances are held every year. More than a hundred years after Sitting Bull, his people still have a strong community. They continue to value their Lakota traditions.

TIMELINE

In the year . . .

1841   Sitting Bull made his first buffalo kill.   Age 10

1845   he counted coup.
his father gave him his adult name—
Tatanka Iyotake, or Sitting Bull.

1856   he was wounded by a Crow warrior in battle.

1868   a peace conference was held in Fort Laramie, Wyoming. Many Plains Indians signed a treaty and moved to reservations.
he and the Hunkpapas moved west to Montana.

1869   he became the main leader of the Lakota people.   Age 38

1872   his warriors fought soldiers protecting railroad surveyors in Montana.

1874   gold was found in the Black Hills of South Dakota.

1876   he took part in the Sun Dance and had a vision of a great battle in which his people would win and all the white soldiers would be killed.   Age 45
the Lakota and other Plains Indians defeated Custer and his men at the Battle of the Little Bighorn on June 25.

1877   he led the Hunkpapas into Canada in May.

1881   he returned to the United States and turned himself in to the United States Army.

1885   he joined Buffalo Bill Cody's Wild West Show.

1890   he was killed on December 15.   Age 59

SHOWMAN

The public was fascinated by Sitting Bull. In 1885, William "Buffalo Bill" Cody hired Sitting Bull to appear in his Wild West Show.

For four months, Sitting Bull traveled to a dozen cities with the circuslike show. He wore the beautifully decorated clothes of a Lakota leader. He had a war bonnet of feathers that reached to the floor. His job was to ride on a fine gray horse in the show's parades. He also sold autographed pictures of himself. He earned $50 a week, plus whatever he could get for his photographs. But he gave all his money away to his people and the poor.

Annie Oakley, the girl sharpshooter, was also in the show. Sitting Bull called her "Little Sure Shot." They became close friends.

When Sitting Bull went back to the reservation, Buffalo Bill gave him the gray horse as a gift. The horse became Sitting Bull's favorite.

FURTHER READING

Adams, McCrea. *Tipi.* **Vero Beach, FL: The Rourke Book Co., 2001.** Colorful illustrations tell the story of how the Plains Indians built and used their tipi homes.

Rose, LaVera. *Grandchildren of the Lakota.* **Minneapolis: Carolrhoda Books, Inc., 1999.** Text and large color photos follow modern Lakota families living on the Rosebud Reservation in South Dakota.

Stein, R. Conrad. *The Battle of the Little Bighorn.* **New York: Children's Press, 1997.** Provides information on the history and people behind the Battle of the Little Bighorn.

WEBSITES

Nativeculture.com
http://www.nativeculture.com This website links visitors to Native American news, events, official tribal websites, and books for young readers.

Tracking the Buffalo
http://www.americanhistory.si.edu/kids/buffalo/index.html This interactive site, sponsored by the National Museum of American History, explains the uses of the buffalo and provides stories, maps, and further reading about the Plains Indians.

The Weekly South Dakotan
www.sd4history.com/index.htm Through this interactive website on the history of South Dakota, visitors can learn about the people, landscape, and events that shaped Sitting Bull's life in the 1800s. Includes timelines, historical photographs, and glossaries of difficult terms.

SELECT BIBLIOGRAPHY

Blaisdell, Robert, ed. *Great Speeches by Native Americans.* Mineola, NY: Dover Publications, 2000.

Eastman, Charles A. *Indian Heroes and Great Chieftains.* Boston: Little, Brown, and Company, 1918.

Malone, Michael P., ed. *Historians and the American West.* Lincoln, NE: University of Nebraska Press, 1983.

Nies, Judith. *Native American History.* New York: Ballantine Books, 1996.

Powers, William K. *Indians of the Northern Plains.* New York: Putnam, 1969.

Standing Bear, Luther. *My People the Sioux.* Lincoln, NE: University of Nebraska Press, 1975.

Utley, Robert M. *The Lance and the Shield: The Life and Times of Sitting Bull.* New York: Ballantine Books, 1993.

Vestal, Stanley. *Sitting Bull: Champion of the Sioux.* Norman, OK: University of Oklahoma Press, 1937.

Viola, Herman J. *It's a Good Day to Die.* Lincoln, NE: University of Nebraska Press, 2001.

Walker, James R. *Lakota Society.* Lincoln, NE: University of Nebraska Press, 1982.

INDEX

Battle of the Little Bighorn, 34, 39, 44
Birth, 5, 8, 44
Black Hills, 27–28, 44
Buffalo, 7, 9, 10, 13, 17, 23, 33, 36, 40, 41

Canada, 35, 36
Childhood, 6–11
Counting coup, 11–12
Custer, George Armstrong, 26–28, 34, 39, 44

Dakota Territory, 5, 17, 28
Death, 43

Family, 7, 11, 13, 37, 38, 42, 43
Fighting, 11–12, 14, 18–20, 25, 32, 34, 43
Followers, 23–24, 42–43
Forts, 15, 21, 38

Ghost Dance, 41–42
Gold, 27, 28
Great Plains, 5, 8–9, 16, 19, 33

Homelands, 8, 27–28, 38

Hunkpapas, 6, 8, 10–13, 15–18, 21, 23, 35, 40
Hunting, 7, 22, 23, 27, 36, 40

Lakota, 5, 8, 23, 24, 27–28, 30, 43
Leader, 5, 22, 24, 30, 39, 42

Montana, 8, 23, 24

Plains Indians, 18, 20–22, 33

Railroad, 24, 26
Reservations, 22–23, 27, 28, 29, 35, 38, 43, 45

Sioux, 8, 22
South Dakota, 8, 43
Sun Dance, 30, 31, 43

Treaties, 21–22, 28, 44

U.S. government, 19–22, 24, 27, 29, 33, 35, 39, 42

Visions, 15, 31, 32

Wild West Show, 40, 44, 45

Acknowledgments

For photographs and artwork: Courtesy Library of Congress, pp. 4 (LC-USZ62-112177), 7 (LC-USZ62-091125), 30 (LC-USZ62-20367), 37 (LC-USZ62-117643), 40 (LC-USZC4-3116), 42 (LC-USZ62-115472); Montana Historical Society, Helena, p. 8; PhotoDisc Royalty Free by Getty Images, p. 10; courtesy Division of Anthropology, American Museum of Natural History Image #50/4243, p. 11; National Anthropological Archives, Smithsonian Institution, pp. 12 (inv 08584300), 22 (inv 01600804), 38 (neg no. 3194-B); South Dakota Historical Society-State Archives, p. 15; The Denver Public Library, Western History Collection, pp. 16, 24; Artist: Carl Ludwig Boeckmann, Minnesota Historical Society, p. 18; National Archives, pp. 21 (NWDNS-111-SC-95986), 28 (NWDNS-77-HQ-264-854), 39 (NWDNS-106-IN-86C); State Historical Society of North Dakota, p. 25; Northern Pacific Railway Company, p. 26; © A.A.M. Van der Heyden/Independent Picture Service, p. 27; courtesy American Museum of Natural History #326847, p. 31; © CORBIS, p. 32; courtesy Southwest Museum, Los Angeles, p. 34; courtesy Center for Western Studies, Augustana College, p. 41. Front cover courtesy Library of Congress. Back cover courtesy of National Anthropological Archives, Smithsonian Institution, inv 08584300.

For quoted material: p. 37, Robert M. Utley, The Lance and the Shield: The Life and Times of Sitting Bull (New York: Ballantine Books, 1993).